616.85 Kub

Kubersky, Rachel

AUTHOR

Anorexia & Bulimia

TITLE

DATE DUE   BORROWER'S NAME

DEMCO

Everything You Need To Know About

EATING DISORDERS

ANOREXIA AND BULIMIA

An eating disorder can make any meal an uncomfortable experience.

• THE NEED TO KNOW LIBRARY •

Everything You Need To Know About

EATING DISORDERS
ANOREXIA AND BULIMIA

Rachel Kubersky, M.P.H.

THE ROSEN PUBLISHING GROUP, INC.
NEW YORK

Published in 1992, 1996, 1998, 1999 by The Rosen Publishing Group, Inc.
29 East 21st Street, New York, NY 10010

Library of Congress Cataloging-in-Publication Data

Kubersky, Rachel.
    Everything you need to know about eating disorders / Rachel Kubersky
(The Need to know library)
    Includes bibliographical references and index.
    Summary: Discusses eating disorders, the role of food in our lives, and how to stay healthy physically and mentally.
    ISBN 0-8239-3078-5
    1. Anorexia nervosa—Juvenile literature. [1. Bulimia—Juvenile literature.
[1. Anorexia nervosa 2. Bulimia. 3. Eating Disorders. 4. Food—Psychological aspects.] I. Title. II. Series.
RC552.A5K83 1998
616.85'26—dc20
                                                                                    91-46600
                                                                                       CIP
                                                                                        AC

Manufactured in the United States of America

Contents

Introduction

*T*ali and Jill have always worn the same size clothes. Yesterday the two girls went shopping for dresses for the junior prom. Tali picked out a black cocktail dress and a long blue evening gown and held them up in front of Jill. "These would look great on you, Jilly! Try them on," she encouraged.

In the dressing room, Jill started to put on the black dress, but she could not pull it down past her waist. She tried a few more times, then gave up. The blue dress was also too tight. It pulled around the hips and waist. "I look like a sausage!" thought Jill.

"Hey—everything okay in there?" Tali called.

"Tal, I don't get it," Jill said. "The dresses don't fit."

"Maybe the sizes are wrong or something," said Tali reassuringly. "Let me try one on."

The black dress fit Tali perfectly.

"Wow," said Jill. "You look amazing."

"Oh, it's probably just a weird style," said Tali. "Let me see the other one."

The blue dress fit Tali too. Jill felt awful. How could she be a bigger size? How come everything still fit Tali? Just a few months ago, she had borrowed Tali's dress for the Christmas party, and it had fit fine!

Jill was quiet for the next hour or so. At lunch, she just had a diet soda. She felt huge and ugly.

"Jill, don't worry. Maybe you're just bloated. It's not as if you're fat," said Tali.

"It's time for a major diet," said Jill.

Jill may be on her way to developing an eating disorder. Teens, especially girls, are at high risk of eating disorders. One reason is the message the media sends that thin is "in." This book discusses two of the most common eating disorders: anorexia nervosa and bulimia nervosa. It explains what these disorders are, why they occur, and what you can do if you or someone you know may be suffering from one of them. This book also explores the importance of food in our society and why so many teens are obsessed with losing weight.

In the 1970s, people were shocked to discover that Karen Carpenter, a well-known pop singer, died of heart failure due to anorexia. Today such stories are far more common. Fortunately, much more is known today about treatment methods for eating disorders. Many of these treatment options have been proven very successful.

Eating disorders can cause serious, permanent physical and emotional damage, but recovery *is* possible. Detection is the key—and the sooner the better. Better still, you can learn to prevent yourself and others from developing an eating disorder in the first place. This book can help you make healthy, informed choices about your body.

For many teens, rituals surrounding food are an important part of being social.

Chapter 1

Food and Your Feelings

A man cannot be too serious about his eating, for food is the force that binds society together.

–Confucius

Food is a necessary part of human life. Human beings need food to survive. Food gives fuel to the body to carry on its normal functions. If your body does not have enough food, it will not work well physically or mentally. If you do not eat for a long period of time, you will die.

Besides its importance for nutrition, food plays other roles in people's lives. To some, food is a source of comfort and pleasure. Memories of grandma's homemade apple pie may bring back happy feelings. For many people, food can also relieve stress and anxiety. Snacking on a sugary cupcake may make you feel better after a bad day. Different foods can symbolize many different things.

Food and Feelings

Food may also influence your emotions. Most of us associate certain foods with certain feelings. For example, some foods may give you the feeling of being cared for. For some people that food might be chicken soup. For others it might be mashed potatoes or macaroni and cheese. Someone else may associate this feeling of safety and well-being with chocolate ice cream or cooked greens.

Foods that make you feel cared for are often called "comfort foods." Your feelings about foods usually develop at an early age.

It is easy to understand why we often associate food with comfort. Your earliest experience with food involved being held, cared for, and fed. Whether you were fed from a bottle or from your mother's breast, you were held close. The good feeling of being held was linked to being fed.

Your need to be fed also made your parents listen to you. When you cried, you told those taking care of you that you were hungry. Then you were not only fed, but also held close.

Food and Traditions

Food and drink, from the earliest times, have played an important part in all sorts of celebrations. Certain sweet spices are used in the baking of Christmas cookies, for example. They are symbols of the gifts of spices that the Wise Men brought to the Infant Jesus.

During the holiday of Hanukkah, people eat potato pancakes fried in oil. The pancakes are fried in oil to celebrate the miracle of one day's supply of oil burning for eight days.

Blackeyed peas, thought to bring good luck in Africa, are still served for that reason on New Year's Eve in some parts of the Caribbean and in the southern United States. And what would Thanksgiving be without turkey and cranberry sauce?

Sharing food with others makes people feel closer. Many people who often eat by themselves say that food tastes much better when eaten with family or friends. People also associate some foods with certain activities. Popcorn may remind you of movie theaters, whereas hot dogs make you think of baseball games.

Your family may have its own food traditions. Joe's mom always made lemon pie for family gatherings. After Joe's mom died suddenly, his dad made the pie. Now, whenever Joe and his family think of lemon pie, they think of the happy times they all shared.

Likes and Dislikes

Have you ever wondered why you crave certain foods when you are upset, sad, lonely, or angry, or why the thought of certain other foods makes you feel sick?

Everyone has his or her own preferences and associations when it comes to food. You may love to eat a particular food simply because you associate it with happy times, as is the case with Joe. When he feels down, lonely, or frustrated, Joe may crave his mother's lemon pie because it reminds him of love and comfort.

Dislikes of specific foods can also develop as a result of emotional events. Joe's ex-girlfriend, Michiko,

recently broke up with him after a three-year relation-
ship. Michiko had introduced Joe to Japanese food, and
the two of them had loved to go to Japanese restaurants together. Now Joe feels sick just from thinking
about Japanese food. The dishes themselves have not
changed, but Joe's feelings about those dishes have. He
connects them with sadness, because he and Michiko
no longer share the meals together.

Food and Stress

Like sadness and loneliness, stress can cause people
to change their eating habits. When under extreme
stress, some people stop eating completely. Others
may eat more than usual. Do you find that you or any
of your friends eat differently during exam period?
Stressed students often eat sweets or junk food in
reaction to anxiety. Others feel too nervous to eat and
avoid food altogether. These tendencies are common
reactions to stress. If you find yourself frequently
relying on over- or undereating as a way to deal with
problems, however, you should know that this behavior can lead to serious, even fatal eating disorders.

Dieting

More and more young women are becoming concerned about body image at an earlier age. According
to a 1997 study in *Pediatrics* magazine, 40 percent of
the nine- and ten-year-old girls interviewed claimed
that they were trying to lose weight. Among teenage

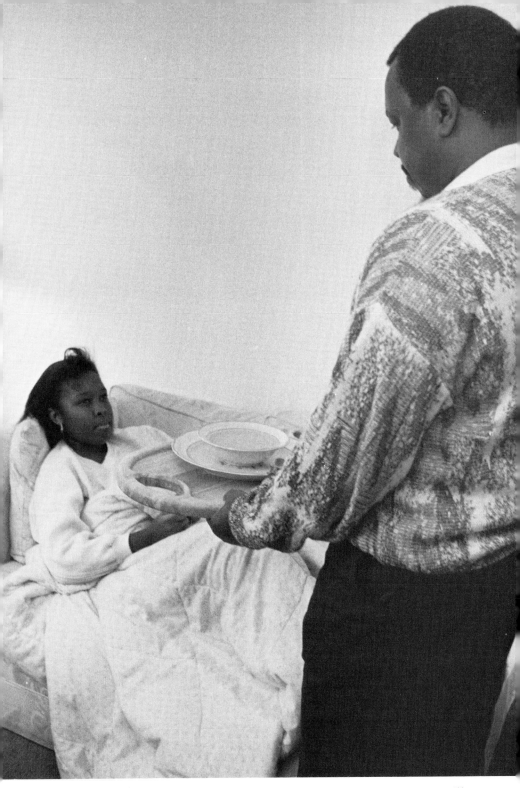

We all have certain foods that comfort us when we are upset or ill.

girls, 77 percent wanted to lose weight, and about 31 percent of women dieted at least once a month. Diets—decisions to limit your food intake to become slimmer—are not necessarily dangerous. The problems begin when sensible choices—decreasing your red meat intake, for example, or choosing low-fat or non-fat alternatives to foods like ice cream and salad dressing—lead to the elimination of foods that provide important vitamins and nutrients. The situation worsens as what began as an effort to become "healthy" turns into an obsession with losing weight. If limiting food intake and getting thinner become the focus of your life, you are in jeopardy of developing an eating disorder like anorexia or bulimia. These disorders, which affect both males and females, can be deadly.

Fasting

Fasting means not eating for a period of time. Partial fasting means that a person avoids eating or drinking certain foods, whereas a complete fast usually means no food or drink at all. Some people fast for political reasons; others fast for religious reasons. When someone does not eat because of political reasons, this is called a hunger strike.

People may also fast for health reasons. These people believe that fasting gives their body a rest from eating and digesting. However, it is important to realize that depriving the body of food for an extended period of time can be dangerous.

Chapter 2

The Weight-Control Craze

Magazines, TV shows, and movies tell us that in order to be successful and happy, we have to be thin. Unfortunately, these messages can convince even the most well-adjusted people that their appearance does not measure up to society's expectations. It is important to note, though, that ideals of beauty vary from culture to culture and from generation to generation. If Marilyn Monroe, *the* movie star of the 1950s, were alive today, she would wear size sixteen clothing. Many stores do not even carry size fourteen!

According to recent studies, anorexia and bulimia are common in the United States, Canada, Sweden, Great Britain, and the Czech Republic—all countries where the "ideal" woman is often portrayed as very thin. In Iran, Egypt, India, and Uganda, where "larger" women are considered beautiful, eating disorders are very rare.

Even within the United States and Canada, beauty ideals vary. Studies indicate that fewer African American teenage girls suffer from eating disorders than their white counterparts. In one study, white and African American males were shown pictures of various female body types and asked to rank them in order of attractiveness. The white males preferred thinner body types with greater frequency than did the African American males.

Many teens feel insecure about their changing bodies. In light of our society's obsession with thinness, these teens may begin to feel that in order to be loved and valued, they must look like the models and actors that they see. Very few people are naturally that thin, however. Many media stars diet or exercise to dangerous extremes and are 10 to 20 percent below healthy body weight. Trying to match this ideal is unhealthy.

Although fourteen-year-old Yezenia was very pretty, had many friends, and had good grades, she was unhappy with herself. She felt fat and ugly compared with the teens on her favorite TV shows. Yezenia decided to become a new, thinner person. She carefully planned her diet: no breakfast, a salad for lunch, and a small dinner.

After a few weeks, friends began to compliment Yezenia on her weight loss. Although the scale said that she had lost twelve pounds, Yezenia still felt huge.

Soon Yezenia's parents became concerned about her moodiness, lack of energy, and refusal to eat anything but vegetables. One day Yezenia collapsed. The emergency-room doctor told her that she suffered from

A distorted body image is nearly always a part of any eating disorder.

Magazines and newspapers are filled with images of thin people who are supposed to be the ideal of beauty for all.

anorexia and referred her to a therapist, a specialist who helps teens with eating disorders. With the aid of the therapist, her parents, and antidepressant medication, Yezenia was on her way to getting better.

Yezenia made arrangements with her teachers so that she wouldn't fall behind in her schoolwork. By the time she was eating normally again and was healthy enough to return to school, Yezenia was so happy to be back with her friends that most of the time, she didn't think much about her weight at all. She found that she had energy for schoolwork and fun activities and even talked to the softball coach and her doctor about joining the team in the spring. Yezenia's doctor told her that as long as she continued to eat healthily and come in for frequent checkups, playing on a team would be a great way to stay in shape.

Where do Yezenia and other teens get the idea that "thin is in"? Messages from the media play a big part, but so does our environment. Teens may be surrounded by friends who talk constantly about dieting, or they may see overweight classmates being teased about their appearance.

When teens compare themselves to models in magazines and actors and actresses on television and in movies, they forget that every individual is different. We each have our own style and taste, and we each have our own unique look. The world would be a pretty dull place if we all looked alike.

Yezenia was able to get on with her life. When she began to return to a normal diet, she found that she had energy again for her friends, her music, and her schoolwork. She gradually learned to be happy with herself and accept that it was okay not to look like magazine models.

Many of our ideas also come from advertisements. We see ads for all sorts of foods and products that promise to make us slim, happy, and beautiful. Health clubs urge us to lose weight. Advertisements almost always show tall, thin, and attractive models.

People in the United States alone spend over $10 billion each year on weight-loss products. These items include diet pills, weight-loss foods and drinks, gym memberships, workout clothing, and expensive exercise machines.

People use these products with the hope of becoming thinner. However, most of them do not want to lose weight to become healthier or stronger. They want to be thinner to be more attractive.

To lose weight sensibly, you need to follow an exercise program and eat a healthy, well-balanced diet. However, if your ultimate goal is weight loss rather than better health, you may resort to unhealthy methods to lose weight. This is how an eating disorder can start. Your goal of losing weight becomes more important than anything else—including your health.

Changing Ideas of Fat and Thin

Where do we get our ideas as to how fat or thin we should be? For the past 25 years it has been fashionable to be thin. Models who wear the latest fashions in magazines have been very thin. "The thinner, the better" is how most people have tended to think about weight and beauty.

But our ideas about fatness and thinness have changed over the years. That is especially true of women's figures. Long ago, for example, it was very fashionable for women to have big hips and big

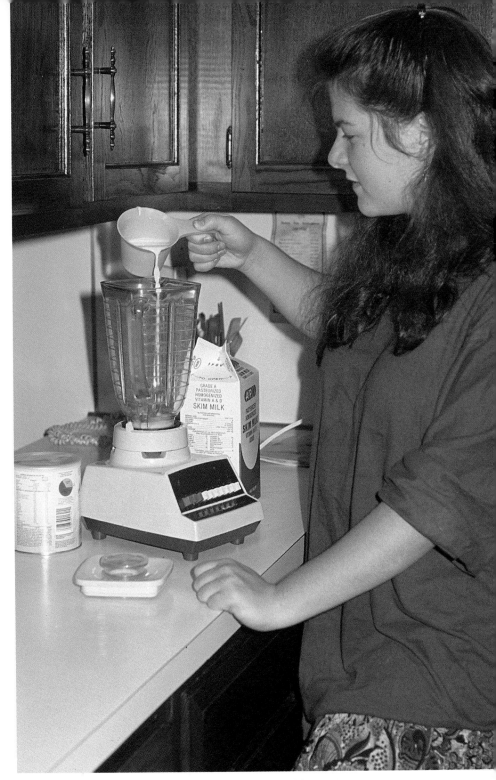

Drastic weight-loss programs can be unhealthy—even dangerous.

breasts. Clothes were designed to show off the hips and breasts.

The words we use to describe body size tend to change, depending on how we think about fatness and thinness. When bigger was more fashionable, we used words like full-figured, plump, and cuddly to describe certain people. Today, those people would probably be called fat.

At one time being heavy was a status symbol. It was hard for many people to get enough to eat each day. If you were fat it meant that you were well off. Thinness was associated with being poor. And because the poor were often sick, being thin was also thought to be unhealthy.

More recently, however, thinness has become desirable. We use words like *slim* and *trim* for a look that in the past would have been described as skeletal and unattractive.

We are influenced by what our culture decides is fat or thin. For some of us that is a big problem. We can't fit into a mold someone else has chosen for us.

The Importance of Healthful Eating

In our drive to become thin, many of us do not eat healthfully. Each of us has a different body type and different food needs. Some people are very active. Some people spend a lot of time sitting down. Some of us are old, some very young. We have different needs at different times in our lives.

A woman who is pregnant needs to eat more than a woman who is not. Athletes who expend a lot of energy have to make sure they eat enough healthful food. When we are recuperating from illness our bodies may require more nourishment to be able to recover completely.

Not eating properly can create health problems. This is especially true of young people. Active young people need well-nourished bodies. Young bodies cannot grow on diet sodas that contain only one calorie.

Plain vegetables and diet soda do not make a healthy, well-rounded meal for a growing teen.

Restricting calories may make you thin, but it will not always be good for you. Dieting too much is more harmful to young bodies than being a little overweight.

Your job as a responsible person is to learn as much about eating healthfully as you can. There are so many things you can eat that are delicious and are good for you. You and your body need to be fed properly.

How Do You Think about Food?

1. When you haven't eaten in a long time, how do you feel physically? Do you feel tired, weak, or even faint?
2. If you are very hungry, how do you feel emotionally? Can you describe those feelings?
3. What food or foods, if any, give you a feeling of being cared for? Do you know why?
4. What are some of your favorite foods associated with family, religious, or national holidays and celebrations?
5. What food or foods, if any, do you strongly dislike? Do you remember when you first developed this dislike?
6. Do you ever eat because you are bored or feeling lonely?
7. Do you know what activities make you want to eat, whether or not you are hungry?
8. Can you name any foods with smells that you associate with certain feelings?
9. Do you ever use food to reward yourself?

Chapter 3

What Are Eating Disorders?

More than eight million people in the United States suffer from eating disorders. Though more than 90 percent of these cases occur in females, the number of males with eating disorders is rising. The two most common eating disorders are anorexia nervosa and bulimia nervosa, which are the subjects of this book.

People suffering from bulimia go through a cycle of bingeing, or consuming large quantities of high-calorie, high-fat foods in short periods of time, and purging, or trying to rid their bodies of the extra calories by vomiting, exercising compulsively, or using laxatives.

Anorexia literally means "lack of appetite," but people with anorexia are actually very hungry almost all of the time. This is because they intentionally eat little or no food, starving themselves in order to lose weight. Anorexics have a severely distorted body image and are terrified of being overweight. Even when they look skeletal to others, people with anorexia continue to deny themselves food because they still believe that they are fat.

Teens develop eating disorders for a variety of

reasons. Many think that if they just lose ten pounds, their lives will be perfect. Teens also frequently develop eating disorders as a way to cope with the vast physical and emotional changes of adolescence. For some, controlling what they eat becomes a way to rebel against and gain independence from their parents. Other teens feel as if their lives are spinning out of control and use strict dieting and exercising regimens as a way to establish some sense of order.

Historical Views of Eating Disorders

A form of what we now call anorexia was seen in the Middle Ages, over 500 years ago. Then it was called *anorexia mirabilis.* The term means a loss of appetite caused by a miracle. In those days many women refused to eat. Their fasting was considered miraculous, and they were considered very special people.

Some religious young women fasted to repent for their sins. They were admired for their ability to survive on the smallest amount of food. One of these women was made a saint. She was called Saint Catherine of Siena. She ate no more than a spoonful of herbs a day. Not eating became a symbol for being especially holy and devout.

Two hundred years later, that kind of fasting was no longer considered miraculous. In fact, it came to be discouraged by the Church. It was thought to be inspired by the devil, so a great effort was made to stop such behavior.

Saint Catherine of Siena expressed her religious devotion by fasting for long periods of time.

In the late 19th century, fasting and starving were looked upon in yet a different way. Science and medicine had made advances. Doctors and scientists were able to identify and name diseases. But they were not yet able to cure them.

Loss of appetite was considered a symptom of many diseases. People were thought to lose their appetite as a result of cancer, stomach diseases, and the nausea of early pregnancy. But few people believed that loss of appetite, or the refusal to eat, could actually be a disease itself.

Doctors found it hard to believe that people would deliberately starve themselves. They felt certain that a separate disease was causing this "lack of appetite." So they kept looking for physical reasons.

Sir William Withey Gull was a well-known English doctor. Around 1870, he came to the conclusion that there was a "starving disease" that began in the patient's mind. He is believed to have been the first person to call the disease anorexia nervosa. The word *nervosa* refers to the mind.

At the same time doctors in France and the United States saw and described similar cases. They came to the same conclusions as Dr. Gull.

Possible Causes

Exactly what causes the mind to "misthink" in this way is still not completely known. There may be many reasons.

Even though anorexics refuse to eat, they will often take
charge of meals for other people.

Some doctors believe that one cause may be not wanting to face adulthood. By keeping his or her body thin, preventing it from growing properly, the person suffering from anorexia (or bulimia) may be expressing a fear of growing up.

Another theory is that people with eating disorders need attention. They see everyone around them struggling with their appetite. They believe that by living on practically no food they can prove themselves to be special and unique. They can feel important and boost their self-esteem.

Many people with eating disorders share certain personality traits. These include low self-esteem, feelings of helplessness or loss of control, and a fear of being fat.

A recent finding suggests that eating disorders may run in families, especially among female members. This may occur because a mother's behavior strongly influences her daughter. Studies show that mothers who place a lot of emphasis on their daughters' weight and appearance increase the risk that their daughters will develop an eating disorder.

Many people also acquire eating disorders to gain a sense of control. They often feel they lack control over their bodies and their lives. In an effort to exercise some power, they become obsessive about when and how much they eat. Another way teens with anorexia exercise control is by cooking for family and friends. This way, they can control what they and others eat.

Adolescence is also a difficult time to establish a positive self-image. Both boys and girls go through dramatic physical changes in a short time. As a teenager, you may see a change every time you look in the mirror. You may also experience a lot of mood swings, or ups and downs.

Sixteen-year-old Adir's parents had fought a lot ever since he could remember, but he never thought it would come to this—his parents were getting a divorce.

Before, whenever the fighting was bad at home, Adir would go for a run. Even during the winter, when the streets were covered in snow, Adir would bundle up and go running. It calmed him down, and by the time he got back, the argument was over.

Since his father had left, Adir had been running more than usual. It was scary to be in the house with his mother, who spent most of her days on the couch watching television or staring out the window. She had taken time off from her job after her husband had left, but it didn't seem as though she was getting ready to go back to work anytime soon. Adir felt sorry for her, but he also felt angry. Some nights she was in a decent mood and called friends on the telephone or asked Adir about school and his friends, but other nights she didn't even leave her room to prepare dinner. Adir would fix sandwiches for them and bring them up to her room, where they would eat in silence.

Soon Adir became obsessed with running. He wanted to become the thinnest, fittest, fastest runner in school. His classmates would admire him, and all

Eating disorders may turn the family dinner table into a battleground.

the girls would have crushes on him. Maybe his father would even come back to witness his son's achievements! Adir read all of the running magazines at the newsstand and carefully studied books on fitness from the library. He wrote up a rigorous training schedule and severely limited his food intake. He skipped breakfast, and lunch was just a piece of fruit and a slice of bread from the cafeteria. It was easy to eat just a few bites of dinner without his mom noticing the leftovers.

After several weeks Adir had lost lots of weight, but he wasn't satisfied. He wanted to be super buff. He decided to add another mile or two to his workouts and to begin weightlifting every day. Yet no matter how much he ran or how little he ate, Adir wasn't content.

He continued to lose weight, dropping from 180 to 125 pounds. But he didn't realize the danger he was in until his mother saw him getting dressed one morning. He looked like a skeleton, with dark circles under his eyes, pale skin, and bones that jutted out of his skin.

Adir's mother was so frightened that she called the family doctor immediately. At the office, Dr. Abraham told them that Adir suffered from an eating disorder and recommended a treatment program for him.

At the treatment center, Adir learned how to eat and exercise in a healthy way. He talked regularly with a therapist about his problems at home and how they were fueling his anorexia. Adir was also able to communicate his feelings to his mother, who began seeing a therapist about her own emotional difficulties.

Dieting becomes dangerous when it rules every minute of your day.

Chapter 4

Anorexia: When Dieting Goes Too Far

Just when you are most confused by all the changes happening in your body as you become an adult, you pick up messages from TV, radio, and magazine ads telling you how you ought to look. The ads are for beautiful skin, thin bodies, silky hair, and long, manicured nails. It is not possible to look like the models in the ads all the time, if ever.

Images from ads probably help bring on eating disorders. But whatever the cause, if you have an eating disorder, you should get help as quickly as possible. That is why it is important to know the symptoms of eating disorders.

The Dieting Fad

You probably know someone on a diet. That person may even be you. The word *diet* used to refer to what someone ate on a regular basis. If you were asked what your diet was like, you were simply being asked what you ate day after day. Today the word usually refers to eating in a special way in order to lose weight.

Dieting has become very fashionable. Many people believe that it is something they ought to do. Dieting is often a topic of conversation.

We have been told so often that thin is good, healthy, and beautiful. But how thin is good? And should everyone be thin?

Fear of being fat makes people, particularly girls and women, limit what they eat. Dieting for weight loss is a serious business. It should never be done without the guidance of a health professional. This is especially true for teenagers. Teens often go on diets to become thin. But the teen years may not be the best time in one's life to diet for the sake of looking thin.

Not eating properly can be bad for your health, especially if you are growing. The food you eat should be carefully chosen. Each meal should be as nourishing as possible. Watching what you eat is important not only for weight loss. It is important because you need to eat well for your body to grow and develop healthily.

It is not easy to be casual about dieting. If you are dieting you may worry about whether you will succeed. You may worry about whether you will look as well as you had hoped after those pounds have disappeared. You may worry about your ability to keep those unwanted pounds off. All that worry can be very stressful.

When people diet they tend to think about it all the time. There is much to do. You have to weigh the food. You have to count calories and substitute some foods for others. You have to shop, cook, and bake. All that effort takes a lot of time and energy.

For some people, dieting can take over their lives. They may feel out of control, which makes them stick even more strictly to their diet. And, if they fail to lose those pounds, they not only may blame the diet, but they will probably blame themselves too. This sort of self-blame is not good for one's self-esteem.

People suffering from anorexia take dieting to extremes. Every waking moment is spent figuring out how to avoid eating. They have to think up excuses to explain why they barely touch their food at the dinner table. Usually they exercise a lot to lose still more weight. Even when they are terribly thin, they see themselves as fat. It is as if the mirror tricks them and lies to them about how they look. In reality, it is their mind that tricks them.

Sixteen-year-old Winnie wanted to be a model. She sent photos of herself to a modeling agency and was called in for an interview. At the agency they said that she needed to lose fifteen pounds. Winnie was told to resend her photos after she lost weight.

Winnie was miserable. She had always thought that she was slim. "Okay, fine," Winnie thought. "They want fifteen pounds, they've got it."

From that day on, all Winnie could think about was her weight. She ate less food and began using diet pills. Even when Winnie had lost fifteen pounds, she didn't like what she saw in the mirror. Winnie's friends began to notice changes in her behavior. She cancelled weekend plans because she didn't want to eat in restaurants—there was no telling how many calories were in each dish, and keeping an exact count was very important to Winnie.

At home, Winnie claimed that she was full after a few mouthfuls of food. Her parents noticed that she was rapidly shedding pounds and looked pale. But since Winnie was keeping up with her schoolwork and seemed to have a lot of energy, her parents assumed that everything was all right.

One day, however, Winnie's mother noticed that her daughter had not touched her tampon supply in months. She became very alarmed and confronted Winnie. When Winnie admitted that she had not gotten her period for several months, her mother called the doctor right away.

It was difficult to persuade Winnie to go to the doctor. Although she now weighed only ninety-five pounds—more than forty pounds below the ideal weight for someone of Winnie's height—Winnie still believed that she needed to be slimmer.

Symptoms of Anorexia Nervosa

As mentioned earlier, there are no early warning signs for anorexia. Weight loss is the first obvious sign. Most of the time we see weight loss as good. So we may actually reinforce a symptom of the disease by complimenting a person who is beginning to be ill with it.

The word anorexia means lack of appetite, but anorexics feel hunger. They may even have severe hunger pangs. But unlike the rest of us, feeling hungry makes them feel good. It reassures them that they are not gaining weight. The worst feeling for an anorexic is feeling full.

Cutting food into very tiny pieces makes it look as though the anorexic is eating.

Many anorexics adopt peculiar habits with food. They may spend a lot of time during a meal cutting food into tiny bites. They may chew the food very slowly. They may constantly drink water. Some of these habits are designed to deceive family and friends. By playing with the food while others eat, they keep busy at the table.

The most visible symptom of anorexia is the large weight loss. But after a while other symptoms appear. The skin becomes extremely dry and pale. The hair becomes brittle. If the person is a female who has begun menstruating, her periods will stop.

Anorexics may also experience frequent light-headedness, even fainting. This is usually the result of anemia. Anemia happens when the blood is not getting enough nourishment to create red cells. It is the red cells in the blood that carry oxygen to all the parts of your body.

As the disease goes on the weight gets lower, the anorexic always feels chilly. Starvation has caused the body temperature to drop. A growth of soft, downy hair develops all over the body. The hair is called *lanugo.* It is the body's way of keeping itself a little warmer.

The brain is starving too. Thinking becomes con-fused and unclear. The anorexic has trouble concen-trating and making decisions.

At this point, the anorexic is very ill and must get help just to survive. Often a long hospital stay is needed to recover.

Chapter 5

Bulimia: The Cycle of Bingeing and Purging

Eating a great deal at one time and them ridding the body of the food is called bulimia. Bulimia is believed to be a modern disease. It was discovered in the 1950s.

Bulimia occurs about twice as often as anorexia. But it is harder to detect. Because they do eat, bulimics do not get as thin as anorexics. Bulimia is less likely to result in death. But it can make you very ill.

The Bulimic Pattern

Bulimics live with a lot of shame. They hate themselves after they binge. Bingeing is the word used to describe the uncontrolled eating of bulimics. When bulimics. When bulimics purge, they tend to feel disgusted with themselves. Purging is getting rid of food, by forcing oneself to vomit, for example.

Like anorexics, bulimics are terrified of being fat. At the same time, however, they have a terrific hunger for food. It is believed that their binge eating may be the result of a hunger of other things that are missing in their lives. Usually, they are not aware of what they are missing.

Some bulimics eat huge quantities of food at one time. Others may not eat that much, but they are always disgusted with themselves for having eaten.

Bulimics make themselves vomit. They also use *laxatives* and *diuretics* (water pills). Bulimics often exercise to extremes to get rid of the food and the pounds. Unlike anorexics, who stay away from food, bulimics need to fill themselves up with food.

Purging is something bulimics must do. It is a kind of addiction. The purging controls them. Because they feel so ashamed of their behavior, bulimics want to keep it a secret. Hiding the binge eating and the purging can demand most of their time and energy.

Getting all that food and eating it without letting family and friends see becomes a real challenge to the bulimic.

Eating huge amounts of food is also expensive. Getting the money for it may become a problem.

Bulimics may have large swings in weight, but their average weight is usually normal. Because they don't look skinny, they hide their disease easily.

Bulimics "binge" by eating a lot of food and then "purge" by causing themselves to vomit.

The Dangers of Bulimia

Bulimic behavior is as dangerous to your health as anorexic starving. Bulimics are less likely to die than are anorexics, but some people with bulimia have choked to death on their own vomit.

Constant vomiting can cause serious physical damage. When a person vomits, large amounts of strong acid are brought up from the stomach. In the stomach, this acid aids the digestion of food, but in the mouth, it destroys tooth enamel and can cause teeth to rot. The gums can also be harmed.

Dehydration from purging leads to dry skin, brittle hair and nails, hair loss, and bleeding gums. Frequent vomiting, which removes food from the body before its nutrients can be absorbed, leads to vitamin and mineral deficiencies. Such deficiencies can cause heart, kidney, and bone problems. They can also lead to a loss of energy that can be very debilitating.

Repeated vomiting can also injure the esophagus— a muscular tube about nine inches long that carries food from the mouth to the stomach—by causing its walls to tear and bleed. If the bleeding cannot be stopped promptly or if a hole develops in the esophagus, death can occur.

Using a combination of diuretics and laxatives can also be fatal. The mineral imbalance that results from the loss of such a large amount of fluid from the body can lead to serious heart and kidney problems.

Between binges, some people with bulimia go

through periods of extreme dieting. They drastically cut the amount of food they eat until they can not diet any longer. Then they begin to eat uncontrollably. Afterward they feel guilty about bingeing and purge themselves of what they have eaten. This ongoing cycle can lead not only to physical damage but also to mental difficulties. Sufferers of bulimia must try to come to terms with their feelings of immense guilt and shame. In addition, since they are constantly hiding how much they eat when they binge, bulimics may become very cunning and often even deceitful. This behavior also leads to psychological problems.

Val, thirteen, was ashamed of her body. She was the only one of her friends who had to wear a bra, and she was already starting to develop hips and thighs. In school the boys teased her about her chest, and the girls whispered about her in the locker room. When Val complained about her body to her mother, her mom reassured her that in a few years, she would be happy to have curves. But Val didn't care about how she would feel later. Right now she felt like a fat cow.

Although Val was going through the normal physical changes of puberty, to her it just looked as though she was getting fat. She decided to diet.

Then Val's older cousin Tamara told her about the perfect solution: She could eat as much as she wanted and then get rid of the extra calories by vomiting and using laxatives. Val tried vomiting and happily realized that it was easy to stick her fingers down her throat.

Soon Val was vomiting and using laxatives every day. But after a few months, she hadn't lost all that much weight, and her breasts and hips only seemed to be getting bigger. She challenged herself to eat as little as possible. For a period of two weeks, she ate only one meal a day, drinking diet soda to satisfy her hunger pangs during the rest of the day.

But one day on the way home from school, Val went to the supermarket to pick up some groceries. Seeing all the food there made her mouth water and her stomach growl uncontrollably. She grabbed some chips, two quarts of ice cream, and a bag of cookies and ate everything within five minutes of arriving home. Then she felt awful and humiliated. How could she be such a pig? She had to get rid of that food.

Val ran to the bathroom and vomited up all the food she had eaten. She had become addicted to the behavior, and it would take a lot of time and work for her to recover.

Val believed that she had found the ideal way to stay thin by purging her body of the food that she ate. Like Val, many of us adopt unhealthy patterns of eating and dieting. When we eat too much of something, we may feel guilty. As a result, we may not eat the next day, or we may exercise too much. Many people fast for a few days when a big party is coming up. That is so they feel they can eat a lot.

Chapter 6

Keeping Your Body Healthy

How do you avoid getting an eating disorder? Unfortunately, there is no *one* thing you can do that will prevent you from getting anorexia nervosa or bulimia. No vaccination or pills can keep you from getting an eating disorder.

Avoiding eating disorders takes a lot of work and awareness; the same things you would do to prevent most illnesses. You have to work at keeping yourself as healthy as you can—not only physically, but mentally healthy too.

Taking Care of Yourself

You have been given this wonderful human being—you—to take care of. This is a job for the rest of your life.

Let's look at how you can take care of your physical health. What does your body need?

You probably learned many ways to avoid getting hurt as you grew up. These reminders may sound familiar:

- Look both ways when crossing the street; cross only when the light is green.
- Buckle up when riding in a car.
- Wear a helmet when skateboarding, bike riding, or motorcycle riding.
- Wear warm clothes in winter.
- Use an effective sunscreen to prevent a summer sunburn.

Another important thing you can do for your health is to have regular medical and dental check-ups. That may help to catch small problems before they become bigger problems. It is always a good idea to ask questions when you visit the doctor and the dentist. Be sure to talk about anything that is bothering you.

Exercise

Exercise is important. It will keep you fit and relaxed. Being physically active can help you let off steam and keep you feeling good. It doesn't matter what you do. It can be playing ball, dancing, running, or doing gymnastics. But it should be something you enjoy.

Always exercise in *moderation*. That means do it sensibly. Don't overdo it. You are in charge. Find out how much exercise is comfortable for you. Know your own limits.

While daily exercise is good, overexercising can cause serious problems of exhaustion, injury, and malnutrition.

Eating Healthfully

Another way to stay healthy is to eat sensibly. What is sensible eating? Here again it is a good idea to follow the road of moderation. Moderation simply means avoiding extremes. It means staying within reasonable limits. Too much of anything is not good for you.

When she was fifteen, Maria decided she would become a vegetarian. She had read that meat contained a lot of fat and cholesterol, so she figured that cutting it out of her diet would be a healthy way to lose weight.

However, after a few months Maria noticed that she was feeling tired all the time. She was horrified to discover that she was losing her hair, too.

Maria's mom made an appointment for her with the family doctor. Her doctor did a blood test. It showed that Maria was iron deficient, which was causing her fatigue and hair loss. Her doctor told her that meat was a good source of iron. He said that when Maria cut it from her diet she didn't eat anything else that provided enough iron. She didn't know it, but she was hurting her body.

Try not to label foods as fat or thin foods. Don't label foods as either bad or good. It is the way we use foods that makes them good or bad for us. There is one exception, however. If you are allergic to a certain food, any amount of that food is bad for you. It could even be deadly. But that is not the case with most foods.

Vary what you eat. We have so many choices of foods. Become an explorer. Promise yourself that you

will try any new food that is offered to you. If you don't
like it, don't ask for more. But if you have not tried it,
you will never know whether you like it or not. If you
don't like a certain food at first, try it again some other
time. Your tastes will change as you get older.

It is not easy to eat right all the time. You may have
a busy life, and it may be hard to eat sensibly at
times. However, your body does a lot of growing and
changing during the teen years. You need to provide it
with a well-balanced diet for it to grow and develop
properly.

A sensible diet is a well-balanced diet. Fruits, vegetables, dairy products, and protein are important to a
growing body. This does not mean you can never have
ice cream or cookies. A sensible diet means that you eat
everything in moderation. If you had a hamburger and
fries for lunch, have a lighter dinner, such as salad and
soup. Try to avoid too much sugar, salt, and caffeine.

Some people say they have problems with snacking.
When we think of snack foods, most of us think of the
commercial snacks that come in packages. Most of
these snacks are actually prepared to tease your taste
buds into eating more than you need. They are very
sweet or very salty, sometimes both. They often contain
a lot of fat. Our taste buds like salty, sweet, and fatty
foods. That is why it is hard to stop eating them.

Snacking itself is not bad. There are times when you
need something between meals. But you can save
money and have snacks that are good for you. If you
have an allowance that you regularly spend on snack

foods, try saving it. Create your snacks with healthier, less expensive foods. Try nuts, fresh fruit, cheese, dried fruit, popcorn, or just plain crackers. Cut up celery sticks, carrot sticks, or any other vegetable you like and snack on that. You know what time of day you usually get hungry. Plan ahead and carry your snack with you.

Think before you eat. That way you will make better choices.

The *way* you eat is also important. Set aside time for relaxed, unhurried eating. Eating slowly will help you to digest your food more easily. It also gives you a chance to make your meals special. Relaxed meals can be a time to look forward to.

Daily family meals—that is, meals eaten at a certain time with most or all family members—have become a thing of the past. Today, family meals generally occur only on special occasions. Some experts believe that this may have encouraged the rise in eating disorders. Do your part in your family to have more meals together. Try to arrange for at least one or two others to eat with you. Let your family know that being together for meals is important to you.

Chapter 7

Your Powerful Mind

You are more than just a body with different parts that have to be looked after. What makes us humans special is that all our parts are affected by everything that goes on in our bodies and in our minds. You not only have to learn to take care of your body, but also to become aware of what is happening in your mind. To avoid eating disorders, you need to stay healthy mentally.

Who Are You?

Get to know yourself. That may sound silly at first. "Of course I know myself," you may say. "After all, I am me."

But you may be surprised at how much you can learn about yourself. It can be an adventure. Try to look at yourself as others might look at you. Try the following exercise. First describe yourself.

Begin by describing your body. What does it look like? Try not to judge yourself. You might even want to draw a picture of yourself.

Next, describe what you are like on the inside. Can you talk about your feelings? Do you know what makes you happy? Do you know what makes you sad? Do you know what you are afraid of? Do you know what you like or dislike?

Then make two lists. Label one, "Things I Like about Myself." Label the other, "Things I Do Not Like about Myself."

On the "Things I Do Not Like" list put an *x* next to the things *you* most want to change. Is your list fair and realistic? Did you put an *x* where you thought *someone else* might want you to change?

You may want to share your list with a friend and have him or her do the same exercise. You may be surprised to see how different you seem to someone else, even to someone who knows you well.

Emphasize the Positive

Many of us are too critical of ourselves. A little self-criticism is all right. It makes us want to change some things about ourselves. But we should not forget all the good things about ourselves.

Remind yourself that you have many good qualities. Give yourself frequent pats on the back. Think about your strengths. Think often about all the things that you do well. Then it will be easier to remember your good qualities when you feel down.

Having a group of close friends can help to ease the emotional pain of dealing with an eating disorder.

Being a teenager is not easy. During this time, you
may have to deal with difficulties in many aspects of
your life. Your body is changing, and it may seem as
if you have no control over these changes. You may
face pressure from friends about how to act, what to
wear, or whom to date. You may also feel pressure
from your family about doing well in school.

You may have a hard time coping with all this
stress, but keep in mind that there is always a solution to every problem. You have family, friends, teachers, and others to whom you can turn for help. No
matter what happens, you are not alone.

Accept yourself as you are. Be kind to yourself. Be
aware of what you can change. Also recognize the
things over which you have no control.

Having Good Friends

Another way in which we grow and learn about
ourselves is by creating relationships with other people. This too can be hard. Friendships take time and
effort. In dealing with friends you can learn a lot
about yourself. Friendships give you a chance to share
both the good times and the bad times.

You have to *be* a friend to *have* a friend. You should
try to avoid being too critical of your friends. Perfect
friends do not exist. There will always be some disap-
pointment and pain in dealing with the people in your
life. But there will also be much satisfaction and joy in
your friendships. If you develop strong friendships,
your friends will be there for you when you need them.

Chapter 8

When You Need Help

Without treatment, 20 percent of serious eating disorder sufferers will die. For those who get help, however, there is a 60 percent recovery rate.

Early detection of anorexia and bulimia is important to successful recovery, so take a few moments to examine the following warning signs:

- Obsession with food and weight: counting calories, excessive dieting, and weighing oneself several times a day
- Claims of feeling fat when weight is normal or even below normal
- Feelings of guilt and shame about eating, not wanting to eat in front of others
- Evidence of binge eating, hoarding food, or use of laxatives and/or diuretics
- Emotional changes, including moodiness, depression, irritability, and social withdrawal
- Amenorrhea (absence of menstrual periods)
- Unusual eating habits, such as cutting foods into tiny pieces or chewing every bite excessively

If you think that you or someone you know has an eating disorder, speak to your parents, a teacher, a school counselor, or a doctor. They will refer you to a clinic or treatment program that specializes in helping people with eating disorders.

At the clinic or treatment center, a doctor will examine you for the following signs: rapid or excessive weight loss, depression or risk of suicide, or severe bingeing and purging. If you show any of these symptoms, you will be admitted to a program immediately as an inpatient. This means that you will live at the facility during your treatment. If you do not show many symptoms, you will be admitted as an outpatient, meaning that you will come to the clinic or center for treatment but will be allowed to live at home.

Both inpatient and outpatient recovery programs focus first on rehabilitating your physical health and then on helping you identify the emotional problems that caused your eating disorder. Trained therapists will help you deal with your feelings.

Many teens with eating disorders are helped by antidepressants such as Prozac, Zoloft, and Paxil. Depression is common among both anorexics and bulimics. If depression is the cause of your eating disorder, taking an antidepressant may help you recover from both your depression and the disorder it has created. Antidepressants may also help by making you generally more open to therapy and to changing your eating habits.

What should you do if you suspect that someone you know is suffering from an eating disorder? Talk to him or her about it—but be sure not to accuse. Let the person know that you are concerned and offer to show him or her information about eating disorders. Many people with bulimia and anorexia are not aware of the dangerous consequences of their behavior. If the person rejects help, do not insist on treatment. If he or she accepts help, be supportive and available. Accompany the person to the doctor's office or clinic. If you feel that you need help, speak to a trusted adult or contact one of the organizations listed at the back of this book.

Above all, remember that eating disorders can be deadly. Anorexia and bulimia can cause permanent damage to the heart, kidneys, and bones. Severe anorexia can cause infertility in women, and bulimia can erode the esophagus so badly that it can be painful for the person to swallow anything, even water. You owe it to yourself and the people you care about to stop eating disorders before they take their toll. Learn and practice healthy eating and exercise habits and teach them to those around you. Most important, try to value people for who they are, not for what they look like.

Where to Go for Help

In the United States

American Anorexia/Bulimia
  Association (AABA)
165 West 46th Street
Suite 1108
New York, NY 10036
(212) 575-6200
Web site: http://www.members
.aol.com/

Anorexia Nervosa and Related
  Eating Disorders, Inc. (ANRED)
P.O. Box 5102
Eugene, OR 97405
(541) 344-1144
Web site: http://www.anred.com

Eating Disorders Awareness and
  Prevention, Inc. (EDAP)
603 Stewart Street
Suite 803
Seattle, WA 98101
(206) 382-3587
Web site: http://members
.aol.com/edapinc

National Association of
  Anorexia and Associated
  Disorders (ANAD)
P.O. Box 7
Highland Park, IL 60035
(847) 831-3438
Web site: http://www.members
.aol.com/anad20

National Eating Disorder
  Organization (NEDO)
445 East Grandille Road
Worthington, OH 43085
(918) 481-4044
Web site: http://www.geocities
.com/HotSprings/5704/edlist.htm

Overeaters Anonymous (OA)
P.O. Box 44020
Rio Rancho, NM 87174-4020
(505) 891-2664
Web site: http://www
.overeatersanonymous.org

In Canada

Anorexia Nervosa and
  Associated Disorders (ANAD)
109-2040 West 12th Street
Vancouver, BC V6J 2G2
(604) 739-2070

The National Eating Disorder
  Information Centre
College Wing, First Floor
Room 211
200 Elizabeth Street
Toronto, ON M5G 2C4
(416) 340-4156

Glossary

adolescence The time from puberty to adulthood.

anorexia nervosa An eating disorder in which a person eats very little food or none at all.

bulimia nervosa An eating disorder in which a person eats huge amounts of food (called bingeing) and then gets rid of it by various ways (called purging).

calorie A unit to measure the energy-producing value of food.

classify To arrange things in a certain way according to subject and category.

culture Beliefs, accomplishments, and behaviors of a group of people, passed on from one generation to another.

diuretic Something that causes someone to urinate more frequently.

epidemic The rapid spread of a disease to many people at the same time.

laxatives Something that causes someone to have more frequent bowel movements.

menstruation The periodic bleeding from the vagina, occurring usually every 28–30 days.

nourishment Food and drink needed for life.

phobia An unexplainable fear of something.

psychologist A person who has studied how the mind works.

puberty The time when the body becomes sexually mature.

recuperate To get back one's health or strength.

rigid Very strict, unchanging, and inflexible.

risk The chance of getting hurt or harmed.

ritual An act that is repeated the same way at regular intervals.

symptom Anything that is a sign of something else.

unique Being the only one of its kind.

For Further Reading

Bode, Janet. *Food Fight: A Guide to Eating Disorders for Preteens and Their Parents.* New York: Simon & Schuster, 1997.

Burby, Liza N. *Bulimia Nervosa: The Secret Cycle of Bingeing and Purging.* New York: Rosen Publishing Group, 1998.

Crook, Marion. *Looking Good: Teenagers and Eating Disorders.* Toronto: NC Press, 1992.

Fraser, Laura. *Losing It: America's Obsession with Weight and the Industry That Feeds on It.* New York: Dutton, 1997.

Hall, Liza F. *Perk! The Story of a Teenager with Bulimia.* Carlsbad, CA: Gurze Books, 1997.

Hesse-Biber, Sharlene. *Am I Thin Enough Yet?* Oxford: Oxford University Press, 1996.

Roth, Geneen. *Breaking Free from Compulsive Eating.* New York: Plume Books, 1993.

Index

About the Author

Rachel Kubersky has a degree in library science and was a school librarian in both primary and junior high schools. Pursuing a lifelong interest in health education, she received a master's degree in public health from New York's Hunter College. Ms. Kubersky lives in Manhattan with her husband.

Photo Credits

Cover photo by Chuck Peterson.
All other photographs by Jill Heisler Hacks, except p. 18 by Stuart Rabinowitz, and p. 27 by North Wind.